AWAKE
THROUGH
DREAMS

Winner of the 2017
Vernice Quebodeaux "Pathways"
Poetry Prize for Women

AWAKE THROUGH DREAMS

CELIA DRILL

FIRST EDITION

Little Red Tree Publishing, LLC,

Layout and Cover Design: Michael Linnard, MCSD
Times New Roman, Trajan Pro, Minion Pro, and Arial.

First Edition, 2018, manufactured in USA
1 2 3 4 5 6 7 8 9 10 LSI 23 22 21 20 19 18 17

Photograph of Celia Drill, on back cover and p.74, is reproduced with kind permission of Lance Drill.

Photographs of flowers on the front cover reproduced with kind permission of the author.

Photographs of the sky on the front cover are public domain images.

Library of Congress Cataloging-in-Publication Data

Names: Drill, Celia, author.
Title: / Awake Through Dreams by Celia Drill
Description: First edition. | North Platte, NE : Little Red Tree
  Publishing, 2018. | Includes index
Identifiers: LCCN 2018146595 | ISBN 9781935656531 (pbk. : alk. paper)
Subjects: LCSH: Collection of poems
Classification: LCC PS3573.I4787 A6 2018 | DDC 811/.54--dc23

Little Red Tree Publishing LLC
509 W 3rd Street,
North Platte, NE 69101
www.littleredtree.com

CONTENTS

"Sometimes I go about pitying myself, and all the while I am being carried across the sky by beautiful clouds."

—Ojibway proverb

"For my part, I know nothing with any certainty, but the sight of the stars makes me dream."

—Vincent Van Gogh

ACKNOWLEDGEMENTS

This book is dedicated to dreamers everywhere.

I would like to thank Bill and Kate Lantry of *Peacock Journal* for their generosity of heart, spirit, and talent, Michael Linnard for taking the time, and spending the energy and resources needed to publish this book, and my guardian angel, the force of nature guiding these poems, for staying true to me all these years.

INTRODUCTION

So there I was, minding my own business, sitting quietly alone in my darkened room. I must have been lost in my own meditative revelry, as I always am, contemplating an ethereal vision, as I always do. I didn't hear the light footfalls coming down the hallway, so I had no warning until the doorknob started to turn. And then suddenly there was Kate, dressed in a new robe, framed by the doorway with the lamplight falling behind her. I didn't see a cast iron frying pan in her hand, but she had one arm behind her back, so I knew it was likely there. Even its unseen presence immediately held my attention.

"William," she said, "You need to write an introduction for Celia Drill's new book."

"OK, darling. First thing tomorrow morning!"

Her voice fell an octave, and strengthened. "Swear me no oaths, and tomorrow me no tomorrows! Now!" I saw a dark curve behind her back: she'd brought the large skillet. I didn't have a good answer. I turned towards my keyboard.

"Introductions are easy to write," I said. "Usually, you just go through the text, find some good lines, sprinkle in a few thoughts, and you're done. It's as easy as baking a blueberry pie."

"So why is this one difficult?" she asked, fingering the skillet's handle.

"George Starbuck told me a good story once. It was a tale of two introductions, the best of his work, and the worst. He was writing an introduction for one of Kinnell's books, I think it was *The Book of Nightmares*, and he wanted to tell everyone how brilliant it was, how they had to sit down with the book this instant, and read it through, two or three times, how it would change their lives."

"How'd that go for him?"

"He said it was the worst introduction he ever wrote. On the other hand, he did one for Anthony Hecht, around the same time. He didn't feel quite the same way about Hecht, so he just wrote a straight, just the facts, description. Looking back, he said it was the best introduction he ever did."

"Ok, William, so do that."

"It's not that easy. Celia's brilliant. There's nothing like her work in all of American poetry. The best analogue for what she writes may be Rimbaud. His *Illuminations* remind me of her work."

"Remind you of her work?"

"Yes. All art is eternally present, and in all languages: '*O terrible frisson des amours novices sur le sol sanglant et par l'hydrogène clarteux ! trouvez Hortense.*' Seek out Hortense. Sometimes, reading her poems, I think her work is what Rimbaud wanted us to find."

"William…"

"I know. But listen to this:

> 'I confess this from my little house, shame box built on stones, poised at the crossroads of the four directions. Animals rush through, all galloping light. Healing. Transforming. In winter I felt the thin walls thicken: chrysalis. In deepest mediation, I have seen myself fly out…'

Or this:

> 'My heart is a woman's heart. Bite into a pomegranate, bloody with seeds, you will taste it.'

Anyone who can write like that has felt the breath of the Goddess!"

"Oh, William, you and the Muse!"

"Do not blaspheme her name! She gives a mantel to the wanderer, and Celia Drill wears that mantle with grace:

> 'The poet in me will never stop walking uncharted paths.'

She almost sails on the wind:

> 'I flew in dresses thin as leaves, a blur of autumn colors.'

And the things she sees and hears on her journey make the world seem alive with the kind of energy Hildegard spoke of:

> 'The flowers have never stood so vivid, have never emanated sweeter spice, nor spoken in such bold voices...'

I think now Hildegard may be a second correlation:

> 'I am only fire passing through this world.'

It's so close to Hildegard's *veriditas*, her *living light*."

"Oh, William, you and your mysticism. Maybe you should write about her prosody instead?"

"That's just as hard. I've spent a lifetime thinking about what poetry is, and how to write it. But even now, her work is still changing my ideas. Try this:

'I placed upon my wall a painting of a door into another home.'

That's exactly it, isn't it: a door into a realm we can only sense. An eternal realm we know must be there. It's what James Wright mentioned:

'At the touch of my hand, the air fills with delicate creatures from the other world.'

And the roses Celia Drill writes of are the gateways to that other world:

'It's good to remember
there's beauty behind the veil, and to know
I could reach through, touch the petals, bring the
wild things home.'"

"Perhaps you're going too far, William."

"Maybe. Or perhaps not far enough. Reading her lines, I can almost feel my own heart as it 'bursts into petals.' Listen to this:

'The moon trills back, flute. Every night of my life, we have sung to each other. Our song is always the same. I intone *be safe. I light a candle for you.* She lilts *Starlight encircles me like angels. I will live forever.*'

This is what makes poems eternal, and she knows it:

'I will never stop singing with the moon.'"

"Wait a minute, William. I thought you were talking about a theory of poetry?"

"I am. Think back to your History of Art classes. Forget, for a moment, all those images of magical beings on the walls of the caves near Lascaux. I'm interested in the image of a hand.

You remember the one: the artist clearly dipped his hand in red ochre and pressed it against the cave wall. All my professors said the same thing: it was a kind of 'Kilroy was here' act. But I think I agree with those who said otherwise. Maybe the image was a material record of visionary experience. And we, who come along later, can place our own hand against the image and share that experience. I think that's how I see her poems: reading them, we can share her experience, and touch that other world she knows so closely:

> 'Much like the heart, the poem can open its doors.
> All the letters fall through. Rivulets of sound stream away.'"

"You have to finish now, William. Do you have a favorite passage?"

"It's so hard to choose. Which is your favorite flower in the garden? Will your favorite today be the same tomorrow? But let's try this:

> 'Stars floating in clouds like breath of white lilac. Like ghosts appearing when all are asleep: they are hungry; they crave earth's music. They want to bed down like rain does in sand, in soil, in the body. In me, empty of all but song and stars.'

Or this:

> 'Within me: starlight drunk while walking night's roads.'

Or this:

> 'I am always listening with the unfurling rose of my inner ear.'"

"These are the things poets truly know. These are the journeys they actually take. These are the things they deeply hear. And Celia Drill is a true poet."

"William, Michael Linnard just wrote to say Celia's been awarded the Vernice Quebodeaux 'Pathways' Poetry Prize for Women 2017."

"That's wonderful news! It's richly deserved. And perhaps this means even more people will hear about her work. Everyone really should sit down with this book right now, and read it through, two or three times. It might just change their lives."

W.F. Lantry
Washington, D.C. 2017

I

THE DREAMING GARDEN

*"It is finally the Wintergarden that produces
the true flowering, the saving vision."*

—Louise Erdrich

*"When the soul lies down in that grass,
the world is too full to talk about."*

—Rumi

Open Fields

"...I am old with wandering through hollow lands and hilly lands..."
—W.B. Yeats, "The Song of Wandering Aengus"

Don't get me started. The poet in me will never stop walking
uncharted paths, through radish and mustard, and all the tall
weeds, their faces haloed, each petal an alm, a stone, a prayer
so easily ripped through by fingers, chewed by caterpillars
green as summer. You tell me I'm making this up, this field
stretching between the freeway and the new buildings, once
four dilapidated houses. You say it's plowed; you say they're
getting ready for cement. I laugh. The flowers have never
stood so vivid, have never emanated sweeter spice, have never
spoken in bolder voices—trills of loved ones, chiming tones of
strangers, purple hearts for faces. There is nothing to do now
but to enter, on foot, at dusk, when the moths invite silver over
each small pool. Here, I am alone. Here, my hair is a single
flame. It is no matter that no one notices, no concern that I am
only fire passing through this world.

Night House

I can see the rose bush from where I sit, high in the balcony's alcove, but she cannot see me. She is a many-armed goddess. I am careful of her, dare not look her in the eye. Her flowers are red as anger, and the breeze singing through her tentacles finds me, makes me drunk and enraged—I storm through the house. One moonless midnight I forged the wildergarden, tried to sever her deepest root, but she was hidden by the mists floating around this house, encircling this village.

She has changed me. My heart glows red as her fistfuls. In full moon's light, you can see it through my chest: complex and many-petaled, the outer layers like the vulva, pink and supine, the inner layers darker, guard a swallowing hole protected by teeth—my heart is a woman's heart. Bite into a pomegranate, bloody with seeds, you will taste it.

Tonight, she is dancing in the migrant wind spilling from the coast, pulling us out of ourselves. Tribal night, generous with stars—paths upon celestial paths spill out, too many to choose. I take one step in each direction, testing; the sky leans forward like a mother, opening her arms.

Perilous moment. I must trust. That nothing will hurt me, not mother, not goddess, not moon. Drunk again, blindfolded by vines, I can step off this edge. If I fall, rose will catch me, claw my skin, cradle my broken bones. If I fly, sky will take me back, moon will guide me.

Black waves of time rush the dimly lit windows. I am night's silhouette, its witch, its daughter.

The Neighbor

The neighbor I have never met calls through my window, says
something about a light shining from my property to hers,
my porchlight piercing her eyes each night through an acre of
forest—an impossibility, though I recall that moon's infinite
arms touch us from light years away, and I remind myself
that even those who arrive unannounced on my doorstep,
touting their much-younger partners, deserve, like all of us, a
basic kindness. I open the door—not the door in the painting
hung on my wall, door of mystery, shrouded by flowers, but
my front door shut like an eye, until they are ushered in,
down the corridors, to the plain grey couch. In an office this
would be the waiting room, but here in my home, it is the
thinking seat, the place one sits to muse on the painting of
the door, to dream of passing into that realm. The neighbors
are too busy for that, even now that they hold glasses of wine.
They finger the glasses like privileged schoolchildren, smirk
slightly as they swill, a private moment between them. And
now they lay out the issues, as if unrolling a scroll: there is the
neighborhood committee's concern over congested parking
near my home, an entrepreneurship she would like my
assistance with, and then, after their glasses are as empty as
before I shared the sour cherried spirits, there is the mention
again of the cursed light, how it must be issuing from beneath
my house, how it nightly finds her window. I imagine she and
her partner compressed in her bedroom, wrapped in black
sheets, staring at the blue curtain, the light lasering a dividing
line between them; he rolls over, crying, like an ashamed son.
Her white hand parts the curtain, her naked eyes probing
the redwoods, those unfeeling sentinels, like men who never
loved her, their bodies harboring the light, reddish like her
disappointment, tinged with blood like the eerie glow of Mars.
Her subconscious blacklists the forest: haunted, and she thinks
she sees my silhouette, witch of the woods pacing her balcony,
her tower—but I am within, seated on the grey couch, my
mind nearly penetrating the door in my painting. I am on the

threshold, inhaling the purple wisteria, ripe as grandmother's lilac-soaked lace. My hand rings the doorbell, and the chime resounds, the cries of wild birds. I freeze, expecting panthers' screams, a cobra's moist slither. The doorknob pulses, radiating heat. From the other world, I hear a woman's voice—is it my mother? Yelling, accusing, sobbing, and then *thud thud thud*: trees' wooden hearts absorbing thrown stones.

The Painting

I placed upon my wall a painting of a door into another home, a white door guarded by vines and flowers. I have stared at it in shadow, gazed at it in window light, wanted to smell the fragrance of the entryway blooms, petunia, rose, gardenia, longed to touch the white paint, not of my own plain wall, but of the door, mysterious and exotic.

Late one night, not sleeping, I turned on the lamp, the lamp with the body of a slender woman, and I watched her saunter, soundlessly, to the door. She knocked so softly with her hand, a lily (she, faceless, behind her large white hat.) I inhaled her perfume and the door's bouquet, one and the same, until the door sprung open. Then, I felt the sweet release of rain's descent, but also the breathlessness of snowfall, as if the air churned powdered sugar.

This was destiny. Like spring becoming summer, summer acquiescing to fall, fall disappearing into winter, her beautiful frailty stepped across the threshold, and the door closed behind her.

A Painting of Poppies

Wild poppies beckon from my pale wall,
my looking glass, mirror of absence.
I enter their realm,
crawl across mud weeping sulfur.
I am a red ant dragging
her dead on her back,
carapace bruised, one foot
maimed in a trap.
I am a caravan of sorrow
listing toward bright flags,
orange as nectarine, melon flesh,
sweet, not bitter, sun, the one I pray to.
Scraping through underbrush, tunneling to light I see
my saviors, my angels floating in a pool
of black water.

Spring

I can take nothing back. But all must be given away. While I speak these words, spring is greening around me, an aura so sonorous it could welcome anyone home. Any interstellar traveler. Or earthly transient. Even the one who never believed he would see another day, now wakes to spring's music: as if the orchestra sits in his living room. Rose and morning glory play duet—intertwine, vine around the windowpanes. He envisions a tawny pony gleaming with pollen, tasting an open meadow, and his childhood wakes. Anxiety, that sour cherry ice, begins to drip, throat to gut. I, too, am throttled by earth's bones stirring, rising. By offerings extended from branch-ends, stem-tips. Who am I to receive these gifts? I who have buried even my jewels and coins, fearing the world's end. While knowing that every word my knife blade pierced in live bark will remain. Tattooed in earth. And the inner wounds I caused, the ones that can't stop talking, are a chatter constant as distant cicadas. I confess this from my little house, shame box built on stones, poised at the crossroads of the four directions. Animals rush through, all galloping light. Healing. Transforming.
In winter I felt the thin walls thicken: chrysalis. In deepest meditation, I have seen myself fly out, dyed the violet of grieving.

Monster in the Garden

Behind the sunflowers, she is getting undressed, all the while wishing she was tall and had blonde hair. She rattles their god-heads until she shakes out the teeth, then eats them one by one, crunching in their shade. This is her day. Her day to be herself. Squat and bleed into the earth if she wishes, lunch on crickets, darken into moon goddess. If only those roses weren't red and beautiful as sin. They make her ugly and poor. And nothing helps her. Makes room for her. The nettle stings. The berries prick. She speaks aloud like reading from a text: *You have forsaken me.* By which she means others like her, rootless, wingless, tailless. By which she means mother, father, sister, brother. By which she means friends, lovers. By which she means self. She wields her scissors, clawing at the bushes. She lops off heads, and they roll to her feet—white of innocence, gold of friendship, pink of first romance. The red rose, real love, resists, its thorns too mighty: her enemy, high priestess of the garden.

Disappearance

In darkness, red roses grow dangerous.
Caress cooling petals
and your hands will pass
into infinite space.

Your body will follow,
grateful to leave the garden,
relieved to be free of tea and conversation.

Floating away, it is easy to see
that the roses were the gateway.

Saint Apple

Lovely green woman—
bounty swells from her limbs,
drops to the feet

of children
who crunch the flesh fresh as water.

Once, I worshipped her
in autumn—

She stood in moonlight,
broad shoulders rippling silver.

I, too, was alone.
I lay on the earth

beneath the rain
of her leaves, her losses.

Pear Tree and the Grown Woman

There is always one who humbles herself: a tangle of green,
down on one knee, while the other storms in, claiming the
air, boorish with sour words, her childhood still swimming in
thunderous eyes. She leans on Pear and knocks at the wood.
Yellow finch flies out, shattering the sonorous humming of
bees. Little leaves rain down, soundless. She pulls at Pear's hair.
Poor Pear, praying to the bountiful body of lake before Fallen
Star wheeled in. Star yells at her children to come to her, her
voice, a man's woken from slumber. Star plucks Pear's fruit,
weaves a crown from the daisies blanketing her roots. Will the
children never come? Star shrinks to the size of a small girl. She
shakes and shakes the branches. Pear gets lost within herself.
She is a mother wandering the prairie, exhausted, children
on her back. And then it is dark. All have gone. She stands
motionless beneath gentle rain.

Lost Orchard

I was born so long ago
that the fertile, flaming peaches
of the trees that nurtured me
have been picked and eaten, picked and eaten
until that beauty is a bare stretch
on the path to the heartland
where little brown flowers peer into gone leaves
and white wolves flow around the trunks
until it snows.

Green Apples

Help me through this. Help me write my way out of this. Hell is this freight of green apples, gaining on me. It's going to overrun me. The men will shove the apples down my throat— I'll be murdered by the thing I loved. Blooming like brides outside my window. I'd blink and see them in my mind: the perfect future, an original, unrequited day in the sun. The air ripe with their crispness. Green apples take me deeper. Further back. Farther away. Become the fruit of certainty. Not of my demise. The roundness in my palm. The child in my womb. Symbol of all living things.

White Cows

I walk toward the fence; the cows walk toward me through the narrowing green. Their identical faces bear my look, the five year old girl in the photograph. She is lost, wildly innocent, but more than that, stricken—ghosts taint the light with murmurs. She listens to the gloom of their conversation, trying to smile.

The cows proceed cautiously, ears perked up. White bodies. White masks. I touch the chilled bones of the gate, just this broken rib between us, fragment of a whole. Here god plants daisies, then plucks out their eyes. Drops stones. Turns grass to serpents.

Forget-Me-Not

Blue, you burn my cheek when you press your flesh to mine.
You are not flowers. You are fingers. Like worms squirming in
air. Reaching toward black earth. Coming up against my face.
Moon, dreaming in grasses, soft white stone. You leave your
mark—scar in the shape of a dark star, shape of a petal.

Poem for My Son

I see him at the edge of my vision:
sunflowers, cornstalks, land aglow
with the born scent of hay.
The place I hadn't known existed.
The secret unearthed. The unasked-for gift.
The realm I turn to now and now
and now and forever and always
while I roam, while I stumble, while I weave
in and out of darkness.

Poppies

I limp in darkness deep as sand. My dog follows, little ghost of
hope, his blue eyes the only color I see. The trees interweave,
one body whose heart has escaped: the moon. Risen far above.
I can hear it beating, soothing distant sisters. In the next world.
The safe place. Where they languish in flowers the color of fire,
the taste of absence of pain.

The Refuge

Job to job to mother-role I flew in dresses thin as leaves, a blur
of autumn colors. Weekly I walked to teach classes, my satchel
heavy with white lies scratched in margins. Statues rested in
the campus outskirts, lonely stairwell strung with vines where
sculptors wrestled clay, cast out disappointments. There in
the heart-brown bushes, the snaking shade, I climbed among
half-hewn animals, misshapen feet and hands, a girl's face
righted in gardenia. Time was precious as her hair, moss-slick,
graveyard-cold: once I loosened my knotted fingers, upended
my wrists, surrender. I dropped to earth, lay my cheek against
the Buddha, his face forlorn, father of the lost. Until bell called,
caged bird hollering. I watched myself rise, rake fingernails
through hair, slap at seedpods clung to hose, wander toward
buildings.

And This, This Was Not a Dream

She was telling me about her father dying, how he was bleeding
from the rectum, and then his liver shut down, and I was
staring at the dandelions, staring hard; we sat in the bleachers—
her son was playing a baseball game. And the next thing
I knew, I was at a saloon, and a woman there said
she just returned from Africa where she helped
orphans with AIDS, and I started to feel the way I had
when the mother was talking about her dad dying—
maybe it was the awkwardness I felt, or how hard it was
to hear, with everyone laughing, pantomiming, behind us.
But I started seeing dandelions, sprouting all over the floor.
They had little manes like actual lions, and they waved
in an artificial wind. It didn't matter whether someone
stepped on them—more sprung up, until the place was filled.
I put my head down, and when I looked up,
everything was gone, swept clean, forever altered.

Love Is a Balloon

The red one close to the ground tries to rise,
but it's caught by the boy with hair like sand—
he smiles and clutches the pale tale, waving it:
No you don't, my dragon, my plaything, my pet—
yet, his sudden letting go
launches one friend into forever,
and the absence twists at this heart
like little sister's pinches—who knew
it would fly so far so fast, and all the while
love him less and less?

There Is Not Enough Love

There is not enough love
in this house, love for
self, yes, but the love
that seeps from the world
and the tears of the soul
is elsewhere, as the daffodil
turns away from us, toward sun.

Creator

You follow me across mountains, places
I haven't yet been, because you are the source
of even my sky. You are rain's fingers
chilling my neck, where I am the young swan
lifting its head to feel your sadness.

As if joy was not born in us. The flowers
flaring in sunlight, sensuous, melon-lush,
heavenly bodies like singing saints

are distant paintings across this wilderness
where I am swan and you are rain.

Gladiola

The tall, red flower
above the black lake

could be my mother
as a girl

at rest,
watching her reflection.

When light strikes her,
she cannot hide

the rich blood
of her emotions. She daydreams

of a boy, determined to marry
to escape her mother.

Soon it will rain
and she will rise,

smoothing the dress
she donned for church.

She will leave the place
where I was

just getting to know her,
just beginning to understand.

Iris Vased Among Roses

I have grown tiresome
though I flaunt velvet, gold-flecked.

I shadow the others,
stooping to disguise my tallness

while sun haunts me
and I flame the color of bruises.

If I were not immobilized,
I would turn away

from the roses clustered in
sisters' conversation.

In their collective pink heart,
in their heady, cloistered air,

I disappear.

Day and Night, the Garden

I think of the owl:

beneath eucalyptus
I met her goddess gaze—

I was prey;
even heart-flutter

caught in the beak, the teeth
of each giant, gold iris.

Since, stacking firewood,
I find eyes
staring through me.

Nights,
I feel like grasshopper
limping over stones,

my bones penetrated
by the lurid lights
of planets.

Muriel

In the patch of foliage
the bonneted woman planted
when she was lonely
and wanting to feel
the cool explosion:
seeds shaken from the packet
to her palms, the heady musculature
of the soil, sun licking her elbow points,
wind caressing the nuance
of her bare neck,
in that sacred place
of longing, that garden—and though
she rests on her bone colored-sofa,
an eye-mask directing her gaze
by increments more deeply inward—
three bucks materialize
to sample her delicacies, nuzzling
the clothesline's cotton dress
now and again with the velvet
of their antlers.

The Spirits Go Fishing in Her Garden

Asleep in the farmhouse parlor,
breezes like gauzy gowns flow in.

I inhale red roses the artist grows,
darkly sweet as wine, as feelings.

All night, I linger at the precipice
where the heart, really does,

it bursts into petals.

I Wake in the Underworld

Above, the winter earth
absorbs last night's rain.
She takes in what she must,
guides it down, down
to roots.

They hold me even now.
I am small and white,
swaddled in the waterfall
of twisted, feeling nerves,

another of the secrets
protected in the birth cords
of the mother.

Preparing for the Afterlife

Like a bulb underground
I am waiting
to leave my body.

I can feel the flower in me,
white as starlight, shape of angel.
She weighs nothing, does not speak.

In her, I release
my secrets: one by one,
red seeds.

Peach Seed's Treatise

Truly all there is
is letting go,
the way a seed must
sprout
somehow knowing
on the other end of its life
it will become
the Godhead
hung with luscious goblets
for the golden, humming masses
rushing toward essence.

Primavera

To open a bud
of the winter magnolia

is to gently lift the eyelid
of your sleeping mother

to make sure
she is still alive

and to see
what she dreams.

Inside the skin,
whorls of wrapped petals

steeped in terrestrial scent
of sapling.

You can kiss them, press them to your cheek,

close your eyes, feel
what she is thinking,

what she is expecting
for her life, for your life.

Awake, a beautiful eye
will look

upon your face,
girl, boy,

woman, man,

whoever you may be
when you discover

your god, your mother.

Forever Flowers

I cast my shadow into the elemental.
My body follows, and we roll
in the roses, the lilies, in the cherry blossoms,
in the lotus, the yucca, in the sanctity of heather,
in the absence of violets, the vibrancy of fuchsia,
in gardenia, dahlia, yellow narcissus,
embracing the within-rain,
the mists and their brides, dancing light,
allowing the fusing of petals,
the quilting of petals to skin,
the giving of breath to wind,
where the heart is a blazing stone.

The Mystic

Beneath mist's thick breath, flowers sway,
lavender and gold. It's good to remember
there's beauty behind the veil, and to know
I could reach through, touch the petals, bring the
wild things home.

Once, I saw a woman at the roadside
picking sweet peas—her car was parked askew,
partly in the road. She faced
the violet tapestry, nuzzling each blossom
the way horses do. I saw a woman

falling in love with herself. Adorned with purity,
how could she do otherwise? I too have searched
mountains for daisies, forests for trillium,
kneeled in high meadows of fairy lanterns, leopard lilies.
In this life,

I've expected little, but held out secret hope,
and so I suppose I have a wandering heart
like the wind that rustles earthly bodies,
like the light that shimmers rarities.
As a girl,

I braved night's fields
to dream with lambs, with daffodils.
Stones and cricket wings went cold.
Everything slept but the stars.

II

SINGING WITH THE MOON

*"There is nothing you can see that is not a flower;
there is nothing you can think that is not the moon."*

—Matuso Basho

"The stars are beautiful because of a flower that cannot be seen."

—Antoine de Saint-Exupery

Stars

The arches of my feet are swollen. Have begun to glow. I am filling up with stars. Like the beasts filled with leaves: within a panda, a bamboo forest. One could shrink to the size of a pearl, drop in, wind along the milky stream to the temple, a hut adorned in bright feathers, steeping in frond-light, where Buddha waits. Within me: starlight drunk while walking night's roads. Across cattle trails where dung steams in mists to highways where the forlorn creep. The stars have gladly flowed into my eyes, my tongue—their bridge to the next world. The finite. Place of rest. Tonight the wind's due course is west. I follow the continent's edge where time mutes and the ocean strikes midnight, commences its homing anthem. To which seagulls respond, followed by egrets, trailed by stars. Stars floating in clouds like breath of white lilac. Like ghosts appearing when all are asleep: they are hungry; they crave earth's music. They want to bed down like rain does in sand, in soil, in the body. In me, empty of all but song and stars.

Singing With the Moon

When night descends on this planet, I am already prone, singing to the moon in my sleep, my voice, the ache of a piccolo—the moon trills back, flute. Every night of my life, we have sung to each other. Our song is always the same. I intone *be safe. I light a candle for you.* She lilts *Starlight encircles me like angels. I will live forever.* She croons; it is me she is worried about. How I try, but often fail. That I continue to age. I beg her to forgive me. For my state of being. I long to be closer to she. More like her. I flatter her, distract her, so she won't pity me. My dreams leap and crash, waves I must swim through or drown, but even churning in brine blackness, I will never stop singing with the moon. Our voices harmonize: piccolo and flute, earth and heaven, servant and master, daughter and mother, lover and beloved.

book

Finally, I began the book that was never meant to be written. The small letters forged the page, each a camel in the desert bearing water for the poor, each word a line of such animals plodding toward a deserving heart. My fingers busied themselves; it felt like invention, but it was transcription—I was a scribe for the muses appearing before me as fairies or dreamscapes or black holes, informing me as I strained toward the page.

I had lived a haunted existence as happily as possible, feeling much like a single white candle flickering in the ether, striving to gain flesh, and to feel the tusks, the trunk, the hide of my own heart, not simply the mists rising from my vapid blood like coolness breathed from rivers—though my enduring emptiness, weightlessness, allowed me to fly each night in my dreams. There the skies throttled me, dyed me blue-black; I woke bruised by divine love like a boat mauled by its ocean again and again, boasting—once it has reached safe harbor—the gashes and the chafing along its battered hull.

Years passed. I don't want to say that I was without hope, because hope was all I had. Hope was the tulip on the table, red wine, the bright marmalade. Hope was the mind straining from succumbing to madness, the pathway from sanity to lunacy just the distance from ear to ear, as the world raged on, my strange race stirring pain into every cup, grinding salt into the sweetness.

And then came the knocking, faint at first, like a tiny person at the door, her whole hand the size of my smallest finger, her knock the whisper from a bird's throat while it sleeps. (I am always listening with the unfurling rose of my inner ear.) The sound grew; it beat and beat. Something was rising: waves, shoots, cries, something was unfolding, smacking its head against the impossible—it smelled like blood, abandonment, rebirth. I was to deliver it.

I washed my face. I wrung my hands. I know what it is like to hold my breath—inhale upon inhale—but to exhale, to surrender, to release deepest breath laced with salt and heat, and to follow where it leads, across lost territories, to begin with words etched across a page, lines of creatures bearing water in their bodies, water bitter with sadness, but purified with promise—that must be the work of another, one braver and stronger than I.

Writing in a Hotel Room

Finally, the solitude
of white sheets, white paper.
One door, closed to the world.
One window, open.
Voices flow in, cleanse my errant thoughts,
like being brushed by wingtips
while falling.

The Heart, the Poem

Much like the heart, the poem can open its doors.
All the letters fall through. Rivulets of sound stream away.
Where they have gone is not important.
It's that the poem still remains.
Just like the heart. It hasn't stopped beating.
It only shed its skin. It let go of all
that was written there. The story inscribed
by the mother and father. The tale
churned out with the blood and the breath.
Behind the words, there was always the heart.
Living in the body like a beautiful child.
Rich with feelings. Brimming over with a story untold.
Bold enough to live forever. Just like the poem.
It is that child, naked before the world.

Inlet, Full Moon

This is the place women come to weep, where gulls rest, shedding feathers. So far from home one has come home. Because the soul never forgets its looking glass. Eyes don't veer from depths. Reflected clouds drift like hands passing over a loved one's face. The motion of polishing stones. A tenderness that makes darkness glow, insects hum, fish rise, bats dive. Time is alive. One's story is being written. Witnessed by the mirrored moon, visage of the beloved.

The Masseuse

Hands don't touch you. Not arms, not elbows. Something else leans over while you lie face down in painted sheets. A presence you must trust or else shrink in shame. Because your body is alone like a branch that has fallen into the river. It is now at the mercy of the flowing of waters, laid bare before the elements, where the sun and the moon prevail, two eyes regarding all that passes. You are blindfolded, rolling beneath the gaze, your skin touched to the bone—it is easy to become hollow, to turn, by moments, more invisible. But you must not, shall not. Masseuse is molding you into a whole self. You will wake tremulous, an aspen enlivened by wind. As you rise, she is sage smoke, hot breath of desert; she is gone.

Desperation Births the Mermaid

Parked in a lot
of burnt grass, broken needles,
I think I see water
swirling, lapping, a night ocean
at my feet.

I step out of my car,
cell that contorts me.
I slip out of my dress,
thin as paper.

There is little left—
my autumn hair, my snow body,
one abalone ring sparkling its sonar,

tugging me, pulling me,
into the waves.

Sausalito

Bring back the black crabs' lair;
They flow over moonlit stones
at the mouth of open sea.

I touch the water
with naked fingers
across continents, the years
a bridge climbing into sky—

I have grown small as a tiny hand.
I have darkened into night of the transparent soul.
I sip salt. Waves of tears flow through me;

I am no longer the weeping girl,
skirts dampened by the tide,
she who climbed the city walls
to mourn the loss of a lover.

The Guests

Whatever was said is lost now. Impressions remain, like washes of pastel color, almost touchable, smelling of cinnamon and warm milk. When I am most innocent, most like a girl leaning against a lavender wall—it could be home, it could be an abandoned building—the dark and light faces of the guests appear, amorphous, angelic, themselves innocents.

The silver car rolls into my driveway, woman bent in the back seat, young boy in front, next to his father, poised as swans. They emerge: father is white, a salt hill. Mother's hair is obsidian paper. The boy twists higher, cajeput-tree, hails from Hawaii. They are foreign to me, like the smell of soft cheeses, shade grown vegetables. Their moon, my moon's sister. Words are exchanged, and with them, our voices, sounds of rough paper and silk that fly off like long-tailed songbirds. The grey light of noon unites us; we are soft as stone.

They stay for days. I hear them below in the flat, sitting in silence of window light; I think she is mending my curtains; I feel her fingers nurture and fine tune the fabric like it is a violin. They come and go in the silver car, calling out for directions through the rolled down window. I descend from the sky to assist.

We build a bonfire in our woods. Standing beneath redwoods, sharing stories, my only son joins us. Speaking across the flames, smiling, our hands gesturing, I imagine continents colliding. Mountains grow—these ashes are seeds for flowers. This future is climbing fields of bronze and rose.

In the end, black hair gentles the tub and sink, where I scrub, and a faint scent pervades, mist of mint: nothing is lost but the words themselves, the words we spoke.

Road to Hana

The goddesses have abandoned us: let vines grow long enough to choke the village, blossoms unfurl like serpents, leaves widen to the size of clouds. Open a window and the breath, the skin of Aphrodite pours in on hot wind: pikake, hibiscus, ginger—she sails over, sails away. Look in the mirror: you won't recognize yourself, gleaming with pheromones, orchid lei around your neck. You are queen of an earth flexing sinew and muscle, a lost time receding into mists. Tonight you'll sleep so deeply you're awake: eyes full moons, yourself the animal, jungle.

Rushing Through These Sacred Woods

A bluebird is mist's eye diving toward forest. Driving below,
I glimpse azure disappear into green, watch mist recede,
recede. Then sun casts veils over the world. Nearly spring, I am
rushing toward a time and place I will soon forget, a meeting
in a building born of crises and deadlines. I choose to conjure
what I already know: there is a heartbeat in each of these trees.
Where a nymph wanders, pine to spruce to redwood, donning
her vine stethoscope. Where she pauses to listen to slow
pulsations, ancient as songs of whales. And what of the stag the
color of Irish mosses? Above the engine's drone, I hear hoof
clap, snort of breath. She gallops, glowing all the spirit's colors.
Where I am the girl riding bareback through the crackle of
pine needles, snow-air flowing through me, fire. My hair, alive
as wings. I am rushing through these sacred woods . . .

Sunny Days

The sky opens. Simple as that. Sunny day, love. Nothing left to dream of. Sailboats circle in the whites of our eyes. Let's cast out. Drink salt. Crunch sinew. Wrap up in skin. Like the seals: roll in warm currents until we are donned in sea. Let's be kings and queens in green, flowing robes, riding the wake of the world.

The Antique Shoppe

To enter here is to step into shadow, then pause to feel the
darkness all around. Having just drunk sunlight, gorgeous
as juice of mangoes. A passage the dead might understand.
The movement from one place, one mind, to the next. Maybe
by choice. Maybe by accident. Arriving nonetheless in the
vortex of dream. Which is why the children hold on tightly to
my hands, their fingers sweating: fawns, nosing my palms. At
this moment so tiny they can sit in the dolls' chairs just inside
the doorway. Little chairs, brittle as little bones. Too small for
Goldilocks, too large for the unborn. Just right for tear-stained
teacups. The children press onward. Rewarded by the dull
gleam of tarnished jewelry, the stale smell of leather misted
with mold. On to rooms stacked with the lost. Jars of bottle
caps, marbles, playing cards. Stop signs, juke boxes, radios,
coca cola coolers. Watchful paintings surround. Portraits of
mallards fleeing hunters. Men and their wives who must have
existed, but surely did not, could not, their faces frozen in
hologram. Real is the bull skull, the exquisitely placed bullet
hole. His still, cold bones draw me, a father's open arms. Below
him, dust motes swirl up like underwater bubbles toward sun.
They permeate the line of his jaw. Fill his eye sockets. Sleep
there like bees in the throats of perfect white lilies.

Shopping

I glimpsed what happens. Within each of us. As we push the carts round and round. I tried not to notice. Tried not to stare. I distracted myself, imagined a meadow punctuated by chirrups of birds. Saw filaments of cloud unite with a cirrus mother, become a beauty, a snow mountain. Steadily she grew, overtook my vision. I touched a woman's palm while picking apples, her fate line broken in the middle. A shadow line inside her life line. We drew back, laughed. I focused as best I could, plucking boxes and cartons from shelves, moving from the coolness of freezers to warm pockets by the bread where I could hear children breathing. I patiently waited while the new checker clumsily scanned each item. I made myself a force field of serenity, a cloud backlit by my own heart, so he could rest his eyes in my direction. I left, shaking my head. Rubbing my hand over my face as if brushing off cobwebs. Trying to recall all that I had seen. It was as if a veil was lifted from each passerby. The thoughts, the messages spoken by the bodies hung lucid as berries from branches. Offerings. Mine for the taking.

Forgetting

I turn and look back.
There is nothing.

Just air, on and on,

a fabric I wrap up in,
long white dress,

its train flowing backwards, to never.

White

The rain turned to snow
before the eyes
of the ten year olds come
from the city to see
just this, this
nothing of a sky
spill out a miracle, as if
the feathers of millions of
never-were birds
floated down, peacefully.
The girl and the boy
opened the car windows,
and their hands were licked
by the space-cold tongues
of invisible stars, or so it seemed
as they flew through the tunnel
of white, through the merging
of day and night, and this was
Earth itself, not television.

Sunrise On the Mountainside, Finding My Father

Years have passed, like rain
abrades the smallest on the mountainside,
tattering the ingrown petals. Among
torn violets, I find you, father, broken
stone crumbling into cold earth, your grains
stolen by winds that sweep the sea.

A life this fractured lies like death,
invites the planet's emptiness to sing:
ice tones tight in the throat, vitriolic
daggers, operatic cries of the mortally wounded—

the song is the white light
strengthening, blinding, a false god
returning to us.

Aubade

Son, your mother kneels before you,
small and grey as a statue of Mary.

Do not pity or worship me,
just rise child, rise.

*

It is like watching earth's star
as it climbs over the land,

as it grows from a single cell
to a heart of fire so great

it could consume the very earth.

The World is Getting Lighter

I have woken up so early the world is still dark.
I would like to go swimming in an azure dream pond,
sunrise rising on wild wings like the realization
that some part of us lives forever
because we are filled with the light of stars.

As I write this, our world is getting lighter
as if I willed it to be, with my desire
for my pale moon to go flying with the blue moon
because they are sisters.

I love how, in silence, the pre-dawn speaks so clearly,
tells me it is dreaming, but soon it will wake, warns me to resist
morning's raptures of joy lest I too soon join the angels.

Betta

This dark room
is night, is the doorway
to the country
where light lives.

I feel sun pulse the circumference,
pierce through, tiny stars,

and the wings
neither of us possess
descend on our frail forms,

woman kneeling over
her disembodied heart.

The Poet

Soon enough,
a woman
with pretty braids
and a wry smile
will walk, a little-
downtrodden,
past wilted bouquets,
names etched on stones,
weeping willows.
Finding at last, that place
to rest, her green eyes
will ferret the gleam
of the light's last rays,
until in cool blue darkness
she'll pull a poem
from her pocket.
Gingerly, as if she's
returning a
handkerchief, she will
place it on my grave.

Winter

The moon found me on a city street,
gliding along in an uncertain dream.
Buildings rose where there were none.
The flooded fields cried out from the places no one lives.
In my hair, in my skin, I felt the child asleep in frozen car,
the woman wedged in battered doorway.
The white egret led me on, swimming in the ancient light
of earth's soul rising.

Crossing

Within a car, I pass over a bridge.
It is midnight, so quiet, the bridge
a man suspended over sea.
I am a dune beetle braving his back,
tracing an ancient path to salt waters.
I would have flown sand winds with the egrets,
our moon a whale's eye open while asleep,
had he not fallen, weary traveler,
heart of pulverized stones,
one of many who perish
on the long journey home

Once, I Held you in my Hand

Stone in the current,
you turn and turn,
exposing your colors,
your natural glitter,
all of your sides;
you rise to the luminous surface,
eclipsing the plane of air,
then drop to the depths
where the crayfish waits, no stranger.

Who is your mother? Who is your father?
You sashay with the minnow,
but you will marry the riverbed,
nest in her warm mud
until the sea takes you, eventually.

Coming of Age

The moon levitated in my window.
I slept pressed to glass, dreamed
she sailed into the garden,
a glowing face
alighting in just-born leaves.
In the morning, I climbed through my window
to find her. I looked
for the woman I wanted to be,
pale dreamer children follow,
the being only animals truly see,
her body a clear pool of water.
I found the depression
where she must have rested
in bright grass still warm.
I lay where she languished,
white lilac all around,
its uberous essence infusing my longing,
breaking my heart.

Begging Spring Moon

Mother, bright as calla fields,
you are gazing at girls, lilies tucked behind their ears,
girls whose bones are growing, whose skin blooms into beauty.
Like night's door opening, like darkness awakening,
you also appear to the women who once were girls on doorsteps
clutching your light to their breasts.
Sway them again on the branches of elms;
sing to them in your voice rattling like seeds.
Let each be sweet in your arms again, tender and perfect:
swan, fawn, lamb.

PREVIOUS PUBLISHING CREDITS

Acknowledgment is made to the following publications where these poems, some in earlier versions, first appeared:

Some of these poems first appeared in:

North Coast Journal: "Muriel."

Peacock Journal: "Open Fields", "Sleeping with the Moon", "Night House", "The Neighbors", "book."

Panoplyzine: "Desperation Births the Mermaid."

Whiskey Island Review: "Lost Orchard."

Perseids: "Love Is a Balloon", "And This, This Was Not A Dream"

Previous Book Published:

Body of Crimson Leaves was published by Backwaters Press, 2006

I N D E X

Poem titles are in bold and first lines in italic.

ABOUT THE AUTHOR

Celia Drill

Celia Drill, (formerly Homesley) grew up in Santa Cruz, CA. She attended Humboldt State University where she studied with the poet Judith Minty and was thrice been awarded the Jodi Stutz Memorial Prize for Poetry. She then went on to obtain her MFA in poetry from San Francisco State University, where she studied with the poet and novelist Frances Mayes. For the last ten years, Drill, a single parent, has worked several jobs, including teaching creative writing at Humboldt State University. Her first collection of poetry, *Body of Crimson Leaves* was published by Backwaters Press in 2006.